JESUS THE

TOLD BY CARINE MACKENZIE
~ ILLUSTRATED BY JEFF ANDERSON ~

BIBLE ALIVE SERIES: PUBLISHED BY CHRISTIAN FOCUS PUBLICATIONS
© 2002 GEANIES HOUSE, FEARN, TAIN, ROSS-SHIRE, IV20 1TW,
SCOTLAND, U.K.

Mary was a poor young woman who lived in the village of Nazareth.

One day an angel came to tell Mary, "You are going to have a baby boy. You will call his name Jesus."

Mary was afraid at first, but the angel told her that the baby was the Son of God.

Joseph was engaged to Mary. When he heard that Mary was expecting a baby, he was worried too. God sent Joseph a message in a dream.

"Do not be afraid to marry Mary. The baby is God's Son. You will call his name Jesus, which means Saviour."

Joseph was happy to marry Mary then.

Mary and Joseph had to travel to Bethlehem to be counted in the country census. Bethlehem was so busy, they could find no room at the inn.

They spent the night in the stable and there baby Jesus was born. He was carefully wrapped up and a manger was used as his cot.

An angel of God appeared to some shepherds in the fields near Bethlehem. "I bring good news. Today a Saviour has been born in Bethlehem."

The shepherds hurried to Bethlehem and found Mary and Joseph and the baby lying in the manger. They praised God and passed on the good news to all they met.

When the baby was
eight days old, he was given the
name Jesus. He was taken to the temple in
Jerusalem and presented to the Lord God.

A godly old man called Simeon held the baby Jesus in his arms. He realised that this baby was the promised Saviour. "I have seen God's salvation," he said.

An old lady called Anna then saw the baby
Jesus. She spent all her time praying.

She gave thanks to God when she met the
special baby Jesus. She passed on the good
news to all the people she met.

Wise men from the East came to the city of Jerusalem looking for the king of the Jews. King Herod was worried about this.

The wise men were guided by a star right to the house where Jesus was. They gave him beautiful gifts of gold, frankincense and myrrh.

They realised that he was the Son of God.

An angel warned Joseph in a dream. "King Herod wants to kill the young child."

Joseph, Mary and Jesus went to live in Egypt until the danger was past.

The family settled in the village of Nazareth where Joseph was a carpenter. Jesus grew up there with his brothers and sisters.

When Jesus was twelve years old he went with his parents to Jerusalem to celebrate the Passover Feast.

When it was time to go home a large party of friends and relations set off back to Nazareth.

After travelling for a day neither Mary nor Joseph could find Jesus. In a panic they hurried back to Jerusalem.

After three days they found him. Jesus was in the temple sitting with the doctors and teachers, talking and asking questions. Everyone was amazed at his answers.

His mother began to scold him but Jesus said, "Did you not know that I must do my Father's business" He was meaning his Father God.

Jesus went back to Nazareth with Mary and Joseph. He was a good, obedient, son. He always pleased God his heavenly Father.

As he grew older he grew even wiser. Jesus said lots of wonderful things. His mother Mary thought about what he said.

Jesus was born to be the Saviour of all who trust in him. He is a good example to us too. He loved to be in the house of God and to do what pleased God.

You can read this story in the Bible in the book of Matthew, chapters 1 and 2, and Luke chapters 1 and 2.